50 Premium Restaurant Pork Dishes

By: Kelly Johnson

Table of Contents

- Slow-Roasted Porchetta with Herb Crust
- Sous Vide Pork Belly with Apple Gastrique
- Iberico Pork Secreto with Chimichurri
- Maple Bourbon Glazed Pork Chops
- Braised Pork Cheeks with Red Wine Reduction
- Pork Tomahawk with Truffle Butter
- Honey Garlic Miso Pork Tenderloin
- Korean BBQ Pork Ribs with Gochujang Glaze
- Crispy Pork Belly Bao Buns with Hoisin Sauce
- Chorizo-Stuffed Pork Loin with Romesco Sauce
- Applewood Smoked Baby Back Ribs
- Classic French Cassoulet with Pork Sausage
- Jamaican Jerk Pork Shoulder with Pineapple Salsa
- Black Garlic & Soy Braised Pork Shank
- Vietnamese Caramelized Pork Belly (Thịt Kho Tàu)
- Argentinian Grilled Pork Asado with Chimichurri
- Sweet & Spicy Thai Basil Pork (Pad Kra Pao Moo)
- Suckling Pig with Crispy Skin & Apple Compote
- Hickory-Smoked Pulled Pork with Carolina Gold Sauce
- Italian Porchetta Sandwich with Salsa Verde
- Shanghai Red-Braised Pork Belly (Hong Shao Rou)
- Spanish Chorizo & Manchego Stuffed Peppers
- Pork Schnitzel with Lemon & Capers
- Barbecue Pork Burnt Ends with Molasses Glaze
- Kurobuta Pork Cutlet with Tonkatsu Sauce
- Portuguese Pork & Clams (Carne de Porco à Alentejana)
- Char Siu BBQ Pork with Sticky Rice
- German Schweinshaxe (Crispy Pork Knuckle)
- Filipino Lechon Kawali with Vinegar Dip
- Pulled Pork Tacos with Chipotle Crema
- Smoked Pork Sausage with Mustard & Sauerkraut
- Apple Cider Braised Pork Shoulder
- Gochujang Glazed Pork Ribs with Sesame Slaw
- Tandoori-Spiced Pork Chops with Raita
- Kahlua Pork with Hawaiian Sweet Rolls

- Seared Pork Tenderloin with Blackberry Reduction
- Pork & Fennel Meatballs in Tomato Sauce
- Miso Marinated Pork Collar with Pickled Vegetables
- Caribbean Mojo Pork with Black Beans & Rice
- Pork Belly Burnt Ends with Smoked Maple Glaze
- Thai Lemongrass Pork Skewers with Peanut Sauce
- Bacon-Wrapped Pork Medallions with Blue Cheese Butter
- Harissa-Spiced Pork Loin with Pomegranate Glaze
- Southern Fried Pork Chops with Buttermilk Gravy
- Italian Osso Buco with Pork Shank & Gremolata
- Hoisin Five-Spice Pork Tenderloin
- Pork Ragu over Handmade Pappardelle
- Korean Doenjang-Braised Pork Belly
- Maple & Mustard Glazed Pork Roast
- Chili Crisp Pork Dumplings with Black Vinegar Sauce

Slow-Roasted Porchetta with Herb Crust

Ingredients:

- 3 lb pork belly, skin-on
- 2 tbsp olive oil
- 4 cloves garlic, minced
- 2 tbsp fresh rosemary, chopped
- 2 tbsp fresh thyme, chopped
- 1 tbsp fennel seeds, crushed
- 1 tsp red pepper flakes
- 1 tsp salt
- 1/2 tsp black pepper

Instructions:

1. Butterfly pork belly and rub with olive oil, garlic, herbs, fennel, red pepper flakes, salt, and black pepper.
2. Roll tightly and tie with butcher's twine. Refrigerate overnight.
3. Roast at 300°F (150°C) for 3 hours, then increase to 450°F (230°C) for 30 minutes to crisp the skin.

Sous Vide Pork Belly with Apple Gastrique

Ingredients:

- 1 lb pork belly
- 1 tsp salt
- 1/2 tsp black pepper
- 2 tbsp olive oil
- **For Apple Gastrique:**
    - 1/2 cup apple cider vinegar
    - 1/4 cup honey
    - 1/4 cup apple juice

Instructions:

1. Season pork belly with salt and pepper, then vacuum seal.
2. Sous vide at 165°F (74°C) for 12 hours. Remove and sear in hot oil until crispy.
3. Simmer vinegar, honey, and apple juice until thick.
4. Serve pork belly with apple gastrique drizzle.

Iberico Pork Secreto with Chimichurri

Ingredients:

- 1 lb Iberico pork secreto
- 1 tsp salt
- 1/2 tsp black pepper
- 1 tbsp olive oil
- **For Chimichurri:**
    - 1/2 cup parsley, chopped
    - 2 cloves garlic, minced
    - 1/4 cup olive oil
    - 1 tbsp red wine vinegar
    - 1/2 tsp red pepper flakes

Instructions:

1. Season pork secreto with salt and pepper, then sear in olive oil for 3 minutes per side.
2. Blend chimichurri ingredients and spoon over sliced pork.

Maple Bourbon Glazed Pork Chops

Ingredients:

- 2 bone-in pork chops
- 1/4 cup maple syrup
- 2 tbsp bourbon
- 1 tbsp Dijon mustard
- 1 tsp soy sauce

Instructions:

1. Sear pork chops in a pan.
2. Mix maple syrup, bourbon, mustard, and soy sauce.
3. Glaze pork chops, then bake at 375°F (190°C) for 10 minutes.

Braised Pork Cheeks with Red Wine Reduction

Ingredients:

- 1 lb pork cheeks
- 1 cup red wine
- 2 cups beef broth
- 1/2 onion, chopped
- 2 cloves garlic, minced
- 1 carrot, chopped
- 1 tbsp butter

Instructions:

1. Sear pork cheeks in butter, then remove.
2. Sauté onion, garlic, and carrot. Add red wine and reduce by half.
3. Add broth and return pork cheeks. Simmer for 2 hours.

Pork Tomahawk with Truffle Butter

Ingredients:

- 2 pork tomahawk chops
- 1 tsp salt
- 1/2 tsp black pepper
- 1 tbsp olive oil
- **For Truffle Butter:**
    - 2 tbsp butter
    - 1/2 tsp truffle oil
    - 1/2 tsp chopped parsley

Instructions:

1. Season pork chops with salt and pepper, then sear in olive oil for 4 minutes per side.
2. Mix butter, truffle oil, and parsley, then melt over pork before serving.

Honey Garlic Miso Pork Tenderloin

Ingredients:

- 1 lb pork tenderloin
- 2 tbsp white miso paste
- 1 tbsp honey
- 1 tbsp soy sauce
- 2 cloves garlic, minced
- 1 tsp ginger, grated

Instructions:

1. Mix miso, honey, soy sauce, garlic, and ginger. Rub onto pork and marinate for 1 hour.
2. Sear pork, then roast at 375°F (190°C) for 20 minutes.

Korean BBQ Pork Ribs with Gochujang Glaze

Ingredients:

- 1 rack pork ribs
- 1/4 cup gochujang (Korean chili paste)
- 2 tbsp soy sauce
- 2 tbsp honey
- 1 tsp sesame oil
- 1 clove garlic, minced

Instructions:

1. Rub ribs with salt and bake at 275°F (135°C) for 2.5 hours.
2. Mix gochujang, soy sauce, honey, sesame oil, and garlic.
3. Glaze ribs and broil for 5 minutes.

Crispy Pork Belly Bao Buns with Hoisin Sauce

Ingredients:

- 1 lb pork belly
- 1 tsp five-spice powder
- 1/2 tsp salt
- **For Bao Buns:**
    - 6 steamed bao buns
    - 1/4 cup hoisin sauce
    - 1/2 cup sliced cucumber
    - 1/4 cup chopped scallions

Instructions:

1. Rub pork belly with five-spice powder and salt. Roast at 300°F (150°C) for 3 hours, then broil until crispy.
2. Slice and serve in bao buns with hoisin sauce, cucumber, and scallions.

Chorizo-Stuffed Pork Loin with Romesco Sauce

Ingredients:

- **For Pork Loin:**
    - 1 lb pork loin, butterflied
    - 1/2 lb Spanish chorizo, crumbled
    - 1/2 cup breadcrumbs
    - 1 clove garlic, minced
    - 1 tbsp olive oil
- **For Romesco Sauce:**
    - 1 roasted red bell pepper
    - 1/4 cup almonds
    - 1 clove garlic
    - 1 tbsp red wine vinegar
    - 2 tbsp olive oil

Instructions:

1. Sauté chorizo, breadcrumbs, and garlic. Spread over butterflied pork loin and roll tightly.
2. Tie with twine and roast at 375°F (190°C) for 40 minutes.
3. Blend all Romesco sauce ingredients. Serve with sliced pork loin.

Applewood Smoked Baby Back Ribs

Ingredients:

- 1 rack baby back ribs
- 1 tbsp salt
- 1 tbsp black pepper
- 1 tbsp brown sugar
- 1 tsp smoked paprika
- 1 cup BBQ sauce
- Applewood chips for smoking

Instructions:

1. Rub ribs with salt, pepper, sugar, and paprika.
2. Smoke with applewood at 225°F (110°C) for 4 hours.
3. Brush with BBQ sauce and grill for 5 minutes before serving.

Classic French Cassoulet with Pork Sausage

Ingredients:

- 1 lb pork sausage
- 1/2 lb pork shoulder, cubed
- 1 cup white beans, soaked overnight
- 1 onion, chopped
- 2 cloves garlic, minced
- 2 cups chicken broth
- 1/2 tsp thyme

Instructions:

1. Brown sausage and pork shoulder in a Dutch oven.
2. Sauté onion and garlic, then add beans, broth, and thyme.
3. Simmer for 2 hours, then broil the top until golden.

Jamaican Jerk Pork Shoulder with Pineapple Salsa

Ingredients:

- **For Pork:**
    - 2 lb pork shoulder
    - 1 tbsp jerk seasoning
    - 1 tbsp soy sauce
    - 1 tbsp lime juice
- **For Pineapple Salsa:**
    - 1 cup pineapple, diced
    - 1/4 cup red onion, chopped
    - 1 tbsp cilantro, chopped

Instructions:

1. Rub pork with jerk seasoning, soy sauce, and lime juice. Marinate for 3 hours.
2. Roast at 325°F (165°C) for 3 hours.
3. Mix salsa ingredients and serve over sliced pork.

Black Garlic & Soy Braised Pork Shank

Ingredients:

- 2 pork shanks
- 2 tbsp black garlic paste
- 1/4 cup soy sauce
- 1/2 cup beef broth
- 1 tbsp rice vinegar
- 2 cloves garlic, minced

Instructions:

1. Sear pork shanks, then remove.
2. Simmer black garlic, soy sauce, broth, vinegar, and garlic.
3. Return shanks and braise at 325°F (165°C) for 3 hours.

Vietnamese Caramelized Pork Belly (Thịt Kho Tàu)

Ingredients:

- 1 lb pork belly, cubed
- 2 tbsp fish sauce
- 2 tbsp brown sugar
- 1/2 cup coconut water
- 2 cloves garlic, minced
- 2 hard-boiled eggs

Instructions:

1. Caramelize sugar in a pan, then add pork and brown.
2. Add fish sauce, coconut water, and garlic. Simmer for 1.5 hours.
3. Add eggs in the last 10 minutes.

Argentinian Grilled Pork Asado with Chimichurri

Ingredients:

- 1 lb pork shoulder steaks
- 1 tsp salt
- 1/2 tsp black pepper
- **For Chimichurri:**
    - 1/2 cup parsley, chopped
    - 2 cloves garlic, minced
    - 1/4 cup olive oil
    - 1 tbsp red wine vinegar

Instructions:

1. Season pork with salt and pepper, then grill for 4 minutes per side.
2. Blend chimichurri ingredients and serve over grilled pork.

Sweet & Spicy Thai Basil Pork (Pad Kra Pao Moo)

Ingredients:

- 1 lb ground pork
- 2 tbsp soy sauce
- 1 tbsp fish sauce
- 1 tbsp oyster sauce
- 1 tsp sugar
- 2 cloves garlic, minced
- 1/2 cup Thai basil leaves
- 1 red chili, sliced

Instructions:

1. Sauté garlic and chili, then add pork.
2. Stir in sauces and sugar, then cook until pork is browned.
3. Add basil and cook for 1 more minute. Serve with rice.

Suckling Pig with Crispy Skin & Apple Compote

Ingredients:

- 1 whole suckling pig (8–10 lbs)
- 1 tbsp salt
- 1 tsp black pepper
- **For Apple Compote:**
    - 2 apples, peeled & diced
    - 1 tbsp brown sugar
    - 1/2 tsp cinnamon

Instructions:

1. Rub pig with salt and pepper. Roast at 350°F (175°C) for 3 hours, increasing to 450°F (230°C) for 30 minutes.
2. Simmer compote ingredients until soft. Serve with crispy pork.

Hickory-Smoked Pulled Pork with Carolina Gold Sauce

Ingredients:

- 2 lb pork shoulder
- 1 tbsp salt
- 1 tbsp black pepper
- Hickory wood for smoking
- **For Carolina Gold Sauce:**
    - 1/2 cup yellow mustard
    - 2 tbsp apple cider vinegar
    - 1 tbsp honey
    - 1 tsp Worcestershire sauce

Instructions:

1. Rub pork with salt and pepper.
2. Smoke with hickory at 225°F (110°C) for 6 hours.
3. Mix sauce ingredients and serve over pulled pork.

Italian Porchetta Sandwich with Salsa Verde

Ingredients:

- **For Porchetta:**
    - 2 lb pork belly
    - 1 tbsp fennel seeds
    - 2 cloves garlic, minced
    - 1 tbsp olive oil
- **For Salsa Verde:**
    - 1/2 cup parsley, chopped
    - 1 tbsp capers
    - 2 tbsp olive oil
    - 1 tsp red wine vinegar
- 4 ciabatta rolls

Instructions:

1. Roll and tie pork belly with fennel, garlic, and olive oil. Roast at 300°F (150°C) for 3 hours, then crisp at 450°F (230°C) for 30 minutes.
2. Blend salsa verde ingredients.
3. Slice porchetta and serve in ciabatta with salsa verde.

Shanghai Red-Braised Pork Belly (Hong Shao Rou)

Ingredients:

- 1 lb pork belly, cubed
- 2 tbsp sugar
- 2 tbsp soy sauce
- 1 tbsp dark soy sauce
- 1/2 cup Shaoxing wine
- 1 star anise
- 1-inch ginger, sliced
- 2 cups water

Instructions:

1. Blanch pork belly in boiling water for 5 minutes, then drain.
2. Melt sugar in a pan until caramelized, then add pork and stir.
3. Add soy sauce, dark soy sauce, wine, star anise, ginger, and water.
4. Simmer for 1.5 hours until tender and glossy.

Spanish Chorizo & Manchego Stuffed Peppers

Ingredients:

- 4 bell peppers, halved
- 1/2 lb Spanish chorizo, diced
- 1/2 cup Manchego cheese, grated
- 1/2 cup cooked rice
- 1/2 tsp smoked paprika
- 1/4 tsp salt

Instructions:

1. Sauté chorizo, then mix with rice, cheese, paprika, and salt.
2. Stuff mixture into pepper halves and bake at 375°F (190°C) for 25 minutes.

Pork Schnitzel with Lemon & Capers

Ingredients:

- 2 pork cutlets, pounded thin
- 1/2 cup flour
- 1 egg, beaten
- 1 cup breadcrumbs
- 2 tbsp butter
- 1 tbsp capers
- 1 lemon, sliced

Instructions:

1. Dredge pork in flour, then egg, then breadcrumbs.
2. Fry in butter until golden brown.
3. Serve with capers and lemon slices.

Barbecue Pork Burnt Ends with Molasses Glaze

Ingredients:

- 1 lb pork belly, cubed
- 1/4 cup BBQ sauce
- 2 tbsp molasses
- 1 tbsp brown sugar
- 1/2 tsp smoked paprika

Instructions:

1. Slow-cook pork belly at 275°F (135°C) for 2 hours.
2. Toss with BBQ sauce, molasses, sugar, and paprika.
3. Broil for 5 minutes until caramelized.

Kurobuta Pork Cutlet with Tonkatsu Sauce

Ingredients:

- 2 Kurobuta pork cutlets
- 1/2 cup flour
- 1 egg, beaten
- 1 cup panko breadcrumbs
- **For Sauce:**
    - 1/4 cup ketchup
    - 1 tbsp Worcestershire sauce
    - 1 tsp soy sauce

Instructions:

1. Dredge pork in flour, egg, then panko.
2. Fry at 350°F (175°C) until golden.
3. Mix sauce ingredients and serve with pork.

Portuguese Pork & Clams (Carne de Porco à Alentejana)

Ingredients:

- 1 lb pork shoulder, cubed
- 1/2 lb clams
- 1/2 cup white wine
- 2 cloves garlic, minced
- 1 tsp paprika
- 1 tbsp olive oil

Instructions:

1. Marinate pork with garlic, paprika, and wine for 1 hour.
2. Sear pork in olive oil, then add clams and cook until they open.

Char Siu BBQ Pork with Sticky Rice

Ingredients:

- 1 lb pork shoulder, sliced
- 1/4 cup hoisin sauce
- 2 tbsp honey
- 1 tbsp soy sauce
- 1 tsp five-spice powder
- 1 cup sticky rice

Instructions:

1. Marinate pork in hoisin, honey, soy sauce, and five-spice powder for 3 hours.
2. Roast at 375°F (190°C) for 30 minutes, basting occasionally.
3. Serve with steamed sticky rice.

German Schweinshaxe (Crispy Pork Knuckle)

Ingredients:

- 1 pork knuckle
- 1 tbsp salt
- 1 tsp black pepper
- 1 tsp caraway seeds
- 1 cup beer

Instructions:

1. Score pork skin and rub with salt, pepper, and caraway seeds.
2. Roast at 350°F (175°C) for 2.5 hours, basting with beer.
3. Increase to 450°F (230°C) for 20 minutes to crisp the skin.

Filipino Lechon Kawali with Vinegar Dip

Ingredients:

- 1 lb pork belly, skin-on
- 1 tbsp salt
- 1/2 tsp black pepper
- Oil for frying
- **For Dip:**
    - 1/4 cup vinegar
    - 1 clove garlic, minced
    - 1/2 tsp chili flakes

Instructions:

1. Boil pork belly with salt and pepper for 1 hour, then chill.
2. Fry in hot oil until crispy.
3. Mix dip ingredients and serve with pork.

Pulled Pork Tacos with Chipotle Crema

Ingredients:

- 1 lb pork shoulder
- 1 tbsp smoked paprika
- 1 tsp cumin
- 1/2 tsp salt
- 6 corn tortillas
- **For Crema:**
    - 1/2 cup sour cream
    - 1 tsp chipotle in adobo

Instructions:

1. Slow-cook pork at 275°F (135°C) for 4 hours with spices. Shred.
2. Mix crema ingredients.
3. Fill tortillas with pork and drizzle with chipotle crema.

Smoked Pork Sausage with Mustard & Sauerkraut

Ingredients:

- 4 smoked pork sausages
- 2 cups sauerkraut
- 1 tbsp butter
- 1 tbsp whole grain mustard
- 1/2 tsp caraway seeds

Instructions:

1. Heat butter in a pan and sauté sauerkraut with caraway seeds for 5 minutes.
2. Grill or pan-sear sausages until heated through.
3. Serve with mustard and sauerkraut.

Apple Cider Braised Pork Shoulder

Ingredients:

- 2 lb pork shoulder
- 2 cups apple cider
- 1 onion, sliced
- 2 cloves garlic, minced
- 1 tsp thyme
- 1/2 tsp cinnamon

Instructions:

1. Sear pork in a Dutch oven, then remove.
2. Sauté onions and garlic, then add cider, thyme, and cinnamon.
3. Return pork and braise at 300°F (150°C) for 3 hours.

Gochujang Glazed Pork Ribs with Sesame Slaw

Ingredients:

- 1 rack pork ribs
- 1/4 cup gochujang (Korean chili paste)
- 2 tbsp soy sauce
- 2 tbsp honey
- **For Slaw:**
    - 1 cup shredded cabbage
    - 1 tbsp rice vinegar
    - 1 tsp sesame oil
    - 1 tbsp sesame seeds

Instructions:

1. Bake ribs at 275°F (135°C) for 2.5 hours.
2. Mix gochujang, soy sauce, and honey, then brush onto ribs. Broil for 5 minutes.
3. Toss slaw ingredients and serve with ribs.

Tandoori-Spiced Pork Chops with Raita

Ingredients:

- 2 pork chops
- 1 tbsp tandoori spice blend
- 1/2 cup yogurt
- 1 tsp lemon juice
- **For Raita:**
    - 1/2 cup yogurt
    - 1/4 cup cucumber, grated
    - 1 tsp mint, chopped

Instructions:

1. Marinate pork in yogurt, tandoori spice, and lemon juice for 1 hour.
2. Grill or pan-sear for 4 minutes per side.
3. Mix raita ingredients and serve with pork.

Kahlua Pork with Hawaiian Sweet Rolls

Ingredients:

- 2 lb pork shoulder
- 1 tbsp sea salt
- 1/2 tsp black pepper
- 1 tbsp liquid smoke
- 6 Hawaiian sweet rolls

Instructions:

1. Rub pork with salt, pepper, and liquid smoke.
2. Slow cook at 300°F (150°C) for 4 hours, then shred.
3. Serve on Hawaiian sweet rolls.

Seared Pork Tenderloin with Blackberry Reduction

Ingredients:

- 1 lb pork tenderloin
- 1/2 tsp salt
- 1/4 tsp black pepper
- 1 tbsp olive oil
- **For Sauce:**
    - 1/2 cup blackberries
    - 1/4 cup balsamic vinegar
    - 1 tbsp honey

Instructions:

1. Sear pork in olive oil, then roast at 375°F (190°C) for 20 minutes.
2. Simmer sauce ingredients until thickened.
3. Slice pork and drizzle with sauce.

Pork & Fennel Meatballs in Tomato Sauce

Ingredients:

- 1 lb ground pork
- 1 tsp fennel seeds
- 1/2 cup breadcrumbs
- 1 egg
- 1/2 tsp salt
- **For Sauce:**
    - 1 can (14.5 oz) diced tomatoes
    - 2 cloves garlic, minced
    - 1/2 tsp oregano

Instructions:

1. Mix meatball ingredients, shape, and bake at 375°F (190°C) for 15 minutes.
2. Simmer sauce ingredients for 10 minutes.
3. Add meatballs and cook for 5 more minutes.

Miso Marinated Pork Collar with Pickled Vegetables

Ingredients:

- 1 lb pork collar
- 2 tbsp white miso paste
- 1 tbsp soy sauce
- 1 tsp honey
- **For Pickled Vegetables:**
    - 1/2 cup carrots, julienned
    - 1/2 cup daikon, julienned
    - 1/4 cup rice vinegar
    - 1 tbsp sugar

Instructions:

1. Marinate pork in miso, soy sauce, and honey for 3 hours.
2. Grill or sear for 4 minutes per side.
3. Pickle vegetables in vinegar and sugar for 30 minutes.
4. Serve pork with pickled vegetables.

Caribbean Mojo Pork with Black Beans & Rice

Ingredients:

- 2 lb pork shoulder
- 1/4 cup orange juice
- 1/4 cup lime juice
- 1 tsp cumin
- 2 cloves garlic, minced
- **For Beans & Rice:**
    - 1 cup black beans, cooked
    - 1 cup rice
    - 1 tsp oregano

Instructions:

1. Marinate pork in orange juice, lime juice, cumin, and garlic for 4 hours.
2. Roast at 300°F (150°C) for 3 hours, then shred.
3. Cook rice and mix with black beans and oregano.

Pork Belly Burnt Ends with Smoked Maple Glaze

Ingredients:

- 1 lb pork belly, cubed
- 1/4 cup maple syrup
- 2 tbsp BBQ sauce
- 1 tbsp smoked paprika

Instructions:

1. Slow-cook pork belly at 275°F (135°C) for 2 hours.
2. Toss with maple syrup, BBQ sauce, and smoked paprika.
3. Broil for 5 minutes until caramelized.

Thai Lemongrass Pork Skewers with Peanut Sauce

Ingredients:

- 1 lb pork shoulder, thinly sliced
- 2 stalks lemongrass, finely minced
- 2 cloves garlic, minced
- 1 tbsp fish sauce
- 1 tbsp soy sauce
- 1 tbsp brown sugar
- **For Peanut Sauce:**
    - 1/4 cup peanut butter
    - 2 tbsp coconut milk
    - 1 tbsp soy sauce
    - 1 tsp lime juice

Instructions:

1. Marinate pork with lemongrass, garlic, fish sauce, soy sauce, and sugar for 1 hour.

2. Thread onto skewers and grill for 3 minutes per side.
3. Mix peanut sauce ingredients and serve alongside skewers.

Bacon-Wrapped Pork Medallions with Blue Cheese Butter

Ingredients:

- 2 pork tenderloin medallions (1-inch thick)
- 2 slices bacon
- 1/2 tsp salt
- 1/4 tsp black pepper
- **For Blue Cheese Butter:**
    - 2 tbsp butter
    - 1 tbsp crumbled blue cheese
    - 1/2 tsp chopped parsley

Instructions:

1. Wrap each pork medallion with bacon and secure with toothpicks.
2. Sear in a pan for 4 minutes per side, then bake at 375°F (190°C) for 10 minutes.
3. Mix butter, blue cheese, and parsley, then melt over the pork.

Harissa-Spiced Pork Loin with Pomegranate Glaze

Ingredients:

- 1 lb pork loin
- 2 tbsp harissa paste
- 1 tbsp olive oil
- 1/2 tsp salt
- **For Glaze:**
    - 1/4 cup pomegranate juice
    - 1 tbsp honey
    - 1 tsp balsamic vinegar

Instructions:

1. Rub pork with harissa, oil, and salt. Roast at 375°F (190°C) for 30 minutes.
2. Simmer glaze ingredients until thickened.
3. Brush glaze over pork before serving.

Southern Fried Pork Chops with Buttermilk Gravy

Ingredients:

- 2 bone-in pork chops
- 1 cup buttermilk
- 1 cup flour
- 1 tsp paprika
- 1/2 tsp salt
- **For Gravy:**
    - 2 tbsp butter
    - 2 tbsp flour
    - 1 cup milk
    - 1/2 tsp black pepper

Instructions:

1. Soak pork chops in buttermilk for 1 hour.
2. Dredge in flour, paprika, and salt. Fry until golden.
3. For gravy, melt butter, whisk in flour, then slowly add milk. Cook until thick.

Italian Osso Buco with Pork Shank & Gremolata

Ingredients:

- 2 pork shanks
- 1 cup beef broth
- 1/2 cup white wine
- 1/2 onion, chopped
- 1 carrot, chopped
- 1 clove garlic, minced
- **For Gremolata:**
    - 1 tbsp chopped parsley
    - 1 tsp lemon zest
    - 1 clove garlic, minced

Instructions:

1. Sear pork shanks in a Dutch oven. Remove.
2. Sauté onion, carrot, and garlic. Add broth and wine, then return shanks.
3. Cover and braise at 325°F (165°C) for 2.5 hours.

4. Mix gremolata ingredients and sprinkle over before serving.

Hoisin Five-Spice Pork Tenderloin

Ingredients:

- 1 lb pork tenderloin
- 2 tbsp hoisin sauce
- 1 tsp five-spice powder
- 1 tbsp soy sauce
- 1 tbsp honey

Instructions:

1. Marinate pork in hoisin, five-spice, soy sauce, and honey for 2 hours.
2. Roast at 375°F (190°C) for 25 minutes, basting halfway.

Pork Ragu over Handmade Pappardelle

Ingredients:

- **For Ragu:**
    - 1 lb pork shoulder, cubed
    - 1 can (14.5 oz) crushed tomatoes
    - 1/2 cup red wine
    - 1 onion, chopped
    - 2 cloves garlic, minced
    - 1/2 tsp oregano
- **For Pasta:**
    - 2 cups flour
    - 2 eggs
    - 1 tbsp olive oil

Instructions:

1. Brown pork in a pot, then remove.

2. Sauté onion and garlic, add wine, tomatoes, and oregano. Return pork and simmer for 2 hours.
3. Mix pasta ingredients, roll out, and cut into pappardelle. Boil for 3 minutes.
4. Serve pasta with ragu.

Korean Doenjang-Braised Pork Belly

Ingredients:

- 1 lb pork belly, sliced
- 2 tbsp doenjang (Korean soybean paste)
- 1 tbsp soy sauce
- 1 tbsp mirin
- 1 tsp sesame oil
- 1 clove garlic, minced

Instructions:

1. Mix doenjang, soy sauce, mirin, sesame oil, and garlic.
2. Braise pork belly in sauce with 1/2 cup water for 1 hour.
3. Reduce sauce until thick before serving.

Maple & Mustard Glazed Pork Roast

Ingredients:

- 1 lb pork loin
- 1/4 cup maple syrup
- 2 tbsp Dijon mustard
- 1 tsp apple cider vinegar
- 1/2 tsp salt

Instructions:

1. Mix maple syrup, mustard, vinegar, and salt.
2. Roast pork at 375°F (190°C) for 30 minutes, basting with glaze.

Chili Crisp Pork Dumplings with Black Vinegar Sauce

Ingredients:

- **For Filling:**
    - 1/2 lb ground pork
    - 1 tbsp soy sauce
    - 1 clove garlic, minced
    - 1/2 tsp chili crisp
- **For Sauce:**
    - 2 tbsp black vinegar
    - 1 tsp soy sauce
    - 1/2 tsp sugar
- 12 dumpling wrappers

Instructions:

1. Mix filling ingredients and place 1 tsp into each dumpling wrapper.
2. Fold and seal, then steam for 8 minutes.
3. Mix sauce ingredients and serve with dumplings.

www.ingramcontent.com/pod-product-compliance
Lightning Source LLC
LaVergne TN
LVHW081501060526
838201LV00056BA/2862